MW00938671

If the Bird

Doesn't

Sing . . .

One person's search for the meaning of leadership

Contents

Preface

Where it all started

During the mid-90's, I was asked to speak at a business class for foreign students at the University of Irvine. The instructor was given my name by someone who had participated in a plant-wide training program that we had just instituted at our TDK Electronics Corporation's audio cassette manufacturing plant in Irvine. The students in the class numbered around 25 or 30. I shared with them my experiences, one story after another, as I struggled to lead the plant to successively higher levels of performance. At the end of this class, I realized I had struck a chord with these students. They appreciated my experience, my candor in admitting that I often found myself perplexed as to what to do next, and, perhaps most of all, how I often made my best decisions from the heart. I found out a month or two later that the class voted me the best speaker of the Speaker's Series, a speaker's forum that involved local business people from the Irvine area. I spoke again the following year, and, once again, the class voted me the best speaker in the series—and again, the third year. I also shared my stories at a business class at Glendale Community College and at

UCLA's lunch speaker series at the Anderson Business School. My stories resonated with these students as well. Of course I was pleased, but I realized that even at this young stage of their careers, these students had a sense of the qualities they wanted to see in their boss, and, they compared and contrasted those positive qualities with their bad experiences that many had already experienced in their young careers. When I sat down to write about my experience at TDK, I thought about these students, and the stories that seemed to touch them.

The Metaphor

"If the Bird Doesn't Sing . . ." is a metaphor based on the personalities of three great leaders in Japanese history. Nobunaga was the first Japanese daimyo, or ruler of a fief, to unite all of Japan, in the late 16th century. It is said, he was an extremely strong and ruthless person. Until Nobunaga's successful unification, Japan had remained a feudal society fragmented into several hundred fiefdoms, often at war. Nobunaga was followed by an equally skillful leader, Hideyoshi. Although Hideyoshi was himself quite ruthless, he had the foresight to begin building an infrastructure to sustain his rule. When Hideyoshi died unexpectedly, he was followed by a very different type of leader—Tokugawa Ieyasu. Ieyasu was the consummate bureaucrat who completed the infrastructure in feudal Japan that ushered in 250 years of peace. The metaphor describes how each of these three great leaders would handle the same situation—how to get a singing bird to sing.

Imagine each of these three great men, seated on a tatami mat, arms folded, eyes closed, with a caged bird hanging overhead from a nearby hook.

"If the bird doesn't sing, Kill it!!!" Nobunaga would shout.

"If the bird doesn't sing" Hideyoshi would loudly exclaim, "Make it sing!"

Finally, "If the bird doesn't sing" Tokugawa Ieyasu would softly say, "Wait until it does."

I'm not sure who first applied this metaphor to a business situation.* The metaphor describes the three stages of business or organizational development. The first stage is the startup, or, for an existing organization, the transformational stage. This is always the most energy consuming stage much like the first stage of a rocket--a large amount of energy is required to overcome gravity, inertia, or, in a business situation, a pervasive malaise and or poor business practices. In this first stage, a very strong hand is needed. You may have to fire poor performers and rally the remaining personnel to work extra hard to get out of this unacceptable circumstance. You must be strong, push hard and act quickly.

*I first saw this metaphor in an article written by Mitz Noda, a senior staff engineer at Hughes Aircraft Company in Culver City, written in a magazine Best of Business, Technological Review, 1979. I read this article in the early 1980's. This metaphor stayed with me for the next 30 years, and, only when I sat down to write this story did it suddenly re-emerge in my mind as a way to structure and describe my experience.

The second stage requires less brute force. A sustainable infrastructure is needed in this stage, where all workers have a clear idea of what they have to do and how to do it (e.g. job descriptions, organizational and function charts). There is a system in place to hold workers accountable in a fair and consistent manner and steps are taken to bring people together to work harmoniously.

Once the infrastructure is solidly in place, an organization can transition into a third stage. In a manufacturing plant, this is the stage where you unleash high performance work teams to continuously improve all important aspects of your manufacturing process and overall organization. Typically, a reward and recognize system is in place with frequent celebrations of individual and group accomplishments. However, never take the foot off of the gas pedal. The organization must continuously improve or go out of business. The 3rd stage infrastructure must be designed to perpetually improve the organization, keeping pace with or, better yet, outpacing the competition.

These are the three stages of an organization. Start-up companies begin at stage one. Companies that are managed by a strongly controlling leader who is reluctant to delegate responsibilities may remain forever mired in stage one. Most companies and organizations eventually go from stage one to stage two. Stage three may remain elusive and impossible to reach to leaders that don't understand the differences between the stages. Each stage could take years, or you may never advance from one stage to the next.

A good leader recognizes the stage of the organization and adjusts his style accordingly. Does the organization require a heavy hand? Does the organization have the structure in place such that the leader can begin empowering the workers to do more with strong supervision? In reality, most organizations in any given stage may have elements and aspects of the stage before or the stage after. A leader must ask, what is missing from the stage we are in and how do

I get the company or organization to the next level. A leader with his head buried in day-to-day activities has little chance to lead the group forward.

I intend no deeper meaning with this metaphor than what I have described above. I say this because the Japanese language is rich with innuendos and deep meanings sometimes hidden from the non-Japanese speaker.

Introduction

My Interview at TDK

Mr. Osugi, a family friend, and an acquaintance of Mr. Tsutsui, arranged my interview with Terry Tsutsui. It was in June 1978. I had participated in judo with Mr. Osugi's son a few years before. Mr. Osugi knew that I went on to study Engineering at UCLA. When he heard that I had graduated, Mr. Osugi called on Mr. Tsutsui, the Plant Manager of TDK's audio cassette manufacturing plant in Irvine. I was a recently married Administrative Assistant with the Psychology Dept. at UCLA. I jumped at the chance to apply for an engineering position. I drove my '63 VW bug from the Westside of Los Angeles, where my wife Carrie and I lived, all the way to Irvine. It must have taken me an hour and 45 minutes at that time of the morning. I was both nervous and excited.

Mr. Tsutsui greeted me warmly and ushered me into his office. It was a small, modest room with a window looking out over the parking lot. Not much of a view for the top executive, I thought.

I quickly handed Mr. Tsutsui my newly drafted resume. I had not held any quality positions up to that point in my work history, therefore, I, in my youthful wisdom, embellished it with quantity—citing numerous part time jobs. My Administrative Assistant position at UCLA was the crown jewel. So I thought. Terry studied my resume carefully. He read each line slowly. After a couple of minutes he moved on to the second page and continued reading at what seemed like a very slow pace. I was a little nervous—anxious to get on with the interview. After what seemed like a very long time, Terry put my resume down and looked at me with his brows knit.

"You have held many jobs." he finally said, with a very serious look on his face.

I nodded, and said yes with a smile, confident that my strategy of substituting quantity for quality had dazzled Mr. Tsutsui.

Terry studied my smiling face for a moment, then he said, "What's the matter with you . . . can't you hold a job?"

Surprised, I stammered, "Uh, er, I . . . I was a student the past few years. Got my B.S. in Engineering at UCLA and my Masters in Sociology at Cal State University of Los Angeles. I worked at a lot of different jobs to pay my way through school."

"Why didn't you say so," Terry responded. He tossed my resume aside and began peppering me with questions, all of them personal and

8

none of them pertaining to my past work experience.

"How old are you?"

"I just turned 30," I answered.

"Are you married?"

"Yes," I said, "just got married last year."

"Any children?"

"Not yet," I replied

"What does your father do for a living?"

"He's a gardener," I responded. And so it went on.

I was being subjected to a Japanese style interview where the objective was to gain an understanding of the applicant's character, rather than exploring his skills and experience. It made sense in my interview, since I lacked the latter. By the interviewing standards of today, this very personal interviewing approach would be viewed unorthodox, if not outright illegal.

Mr. Tsutsui asked me to describe myself. As a Japanese American, raised a Buddhist, I found it extremely difficult to "sell myself" to him.* Instead, I droned on in a very objective and non-flattering way. At one point while I was talking, Terry leaned back in his swivel chair, tilted his head back and closed his eyes. He even rubbed the bridge of his nose, also with his eyes closed, as I continued to talk.

Damn, I thought. He's falling asleep. Perhaps he was just in deep thought. I wasn't quite sure. Finally, he sat up, asked a couple of more questions, and we ended the interview with details about my pay. He was going to pay me $7 per hour. It appeared that I was hired, but doing what?

---

*My wife and I are members of *Senshin* Buddhist Temple located near the campus of USC. Our Reverend Mas Kodani has given several sermons explaining how difficult it is for Japanese Americans, especially JA's raised as Buddhist, to "sell themselves" in an interview for a job, or college entrance. I believe he is correct. It feels extremely awkward to cite ones accomplishments or good points. I wasn't sure why until Reverend Kodani explained that we are taught to be humble and not exaggerate our self-importance. Most of us in this situation don't even realize why we feel so uncomfortable when asked to cite our accomplishments. Therefore, we can be at a disadvantage when we are put in a situation such as a job interview.

"$7.00 per hour as an industrial engineer?" I asked.

"No," he said. Not as an engineer. I don't know what you will be doing yet. I'll figure it out. Come back on Monday at 8 a.m. and be ready to work.

"Where will I sit? Who will I report to? What will I be doing?"

"I'll show you," Terry said. "You will report directly to me."

And so began my 29 year career with TDK. During those first few years I did everything that the Japanese didn't want to do, and I did them gladly. I soaked up the responsibilities and loved every minute. Terry was doubling as the purchasing agent and he was more than happy to turn that role over to me. Mr. Noguchi, the Quality Assurance manager, was doing double duty as the master production scheduler. He couldn't wait to unload that on me. I worked without a job title for the first year and half. In fact, I gave myself my first job title when I was given the task of writing job descriptions for all the workers. By this time, Sam Koizumi replaced Terry Tsutsui as the Plant Manager. Sam promoted me to Assistant Manager of Production Control and Purchasing.

After a few years I was promoted to manager, and shortly after that, I became the Director of Production Control and Purchasing. The plant now had seven audio assembly lines that cranked out 10 million audio cassettes per month. There was a complement of molding machines that created the halves (two sides of the cassette). The assembly line inserted the components into the halves, closed it, and then automatically screwed the two sides together. We also had a complement of molding machines that made the p-cases in which the cassettes were inserted before they were packaged. Two high speed packaging lines met our needs. There was even talk of adding micro floppy disc production to our plant operations. I was excited about the prospect of adding a new product to our operation. As a director who reported to the Plant Manager, I thought I had gone as far as I could in this organization.   I was sure that the Plant Manager and the Finance Director would always be a Japanese from the main TDK operation in Japan.

After all, TDK was a Japanese company with a history dating back to the 1930's.*

*TDK had a long history of successful manufacturing in Japan, with a strong commitment to producing high quality products. The company was extremely well managed and annually voted among the top ten most financially sound companies in Japan. I will not be describing the TDK manufacturing technique since this is proprietary information.   Students of manufacturing would be wise to study Six Sigma, Lean Manufacturing or any of the other currently popular methods of managing production. This paper will focus on leadership and how to harness the power of the workforce.

Chapter One:

If the bird doesn't sing . . .
kill it!!!

Getting the organization on the right track

"Good news and bad news"

It was around September of 1991. After a series of long meetings, most of which were in Japanese, and little of which was translated into English, Mr. Kuwajima called for a break. Mr. Kuwajima was a Jigyo Bucho, or J.B., a title given to a high ranking director or a position just below Board of Director. Looking much younger than his years, perhaps because of his jet black hair, Mr. Kuwajima was a mild mannered, but extremely hard working man. I wasn't quite sure why he was here at our plant. My guess was that he came to the California Plant to see first-hand how our plant was operating and to discuss future goals with Mr. Takei, the Plant Manager. KC Yanagisawa accompanied Mr. Kuwajima. KC had previously worked at our plant as the QA Manager. After a few years in California, KC was transferred to TDK Georgia where he worked as the QA Manager for the Georgia Video Plant. After his stint in Georgia, KC was reassigned to Japan. He was accompanying Mr. Kuwajima, I presumed, because KC was so familiar with our audio plant, and, KC spoke English fluently.

KC asked me to join him in the cafeteria for coffee. Mr. Kuwajima, KC and I sat at a table. No one else was in the room. KC was a bit of a jokester—very bright, and given to cracking jokes. However, no one was talking when we first sat down. I saw KC look at Mr. Kuwajima, who then gave a nod as if to signal, go ahead and speak.

KC looked at me and began, "I have good news and bad news."

I was expecting a KC joke.

KC continued, "The good news is, you're going to be the next Plant Manager."

I was stunned. I did not see this coming. For a brief moment I felt awed and elated.

KC continued, "But the bad news is, if you don't turn California Plant around and turn it around quickly, you will be the last Plant Manager."

Over the years I thought about how KC delivered this announcement. First, he did me a huge favor by describing the situation clearly and directly. Japanese often speak in ways that are subtle with different levels of meaning, many of which can go undetected by someone not Japanese. It is said that when a Japanese states one thing, he implies nine others. Even with my Japanese American upbringing, I guess that I could discern less than half of what was implied.

KC explained the California Plant situation further. "As you know, we have started construction of an audio tape plant in Thailand. On paper, we think that the Thailand plant's factory cost will be so much lower than yours that it would make good business sense to close down the California Plant and move all of the audio production to Thailand."

As I listened to KC's explanation, my brief feeling of joy disappeared and it was replaced by an overwhelming sense of responsibility— responsibility for the welfare of the 300 or so employees that would be working for me. Up to that point in my career, only about 10% or 30 employees worked under my area of responsibility. I was now to become the new leader of everyone in the plant. Their careers would rest in my hands. This huge sense of responsibility stayed with me for the rest of my career with TDK.

In conclusion, KC said, "You have to bring the factory cost down and down very quickly. If you do not bring it down, or bring it down quickly enough, your plant will be closed. Do you understand?"

"Yes. You made it very clear." I answered.

Mr. Kuwajima, who was listening attentively, said something to KC in Japanese that I didn't completely understand.

KC turned to me and said, "Oh, by the way, congratulations."

The three of us laughed.

"Thank you." I said. "When will I start? When will Mr. Takei be returning to Japan?"

"We're not sure," KC answered. "Mr. Takei may return in March of next year, but you should get started right away."

We finished our coffee and returned to our meeting. The next day, KC announced my appointment as the next Plant Manager. I always thought that a Japanese would fill the Plant Manager position. During the announcement, KC said that as far as he knew, I was the first non-Japanese to head a TDK plant.* I hope I'm not the last, I thought to myself.

---

*By 1992, TDK had emerged as a world leader in the manufacturing of ferrite components and magnetic media, e.g., audio cassettes, video cassettes and early research into compact discs and digital compact discs. TDK had over a dozen plants worldwide with an annual sale of over $5 billion dollars. TDK California was the first TDK manufacturing plant built in the U.S., opening its doors in 1973.

To help me get off to a good start, TDK headquarters sent Kuni Matsui to our plant. Kuni was a very bright and gifted manager who had worked at TDK New York for a number of years. Although born and raised in Japan, Kuni loved the U.S. and received his bachelor's degree from Colorado State University. He was totally fluent in English and experienced working with Americans. Kuni was the first of the truly talented partners I would gain to help me manage the plant. His primary role was to act as the plant liaison to TDK Japan. He was then and continued to be an indispensable friend and ally.

Mr. Takei

Mr. Takei was the Plant Manager when KC and Mr. Kuwajima informed me that I would be the next leader of the plant. Mr. Takei loved the U.S. He loved his assignment. He loved his work, and, while I didn't know the circumstances for his being reassigned back to Japan, I did know that he didn't want to go back. He had a great deal of freedom in the U.S. I thought he ran the plant well and the workers, including me, liked him very much. However, the relationship between Mr. Takei and I became strained after KC and Mr. Kuwajima returned to Japan. I wasn't sure why. It was September 1991, and Mr. Takei was not scheduled to leave until March 1992. TDK's business year was from April through March, therefore, most major organizational changes began in April.

All of the Japanese expatriates at the California Plant rallied around me. At that time, there were more than 20. Most of them were engineers. In management, there was a Japanese Accounting Manager, Taka Ono, and there was Kuni.

We needed to set the stage for the transition of leadership as quickly as possible. We did not want to wait until Mr. Takei returned to Japan. We were preparing to add micro floppy disc (MFD) production to our manufacturing product line, and we needed to make sure that we had good managers and supervisors. The problem was that no one (in Japan) considered that the plant now had two leaders, Mr. Takei and I. Mr. Takei was holding his own set of meetings as if nothing had changed.

On an unusually hot day in November, a group of about 30 managers and Japanese engineers met in a stuffy office on the 2nd floor of our warehouse, down the street from the audio plant. It was awkward to meet in this location, but the thinking was that it would be more awkward if we met in the audio building with Mr. Takei there. We were working on the organizational chart that we hoped to kick into place in January. Getting our micro floppy disc operation off to a strong start was a priority and critical for our future. We needed a strong organization for the MFD production area if we hoped to remain competitive in the U.S. market.

Our discussion had come to a stalemate. We were hopelessly stuck. We had to be careful not to pull too many strong managers and supervisors away from audio production. How to strengthen one area without weakening the other? After an hour of discussion we were going nowhere. Feeling hot and uncomfortable, I got up, copied the chart on our copy board, informed the group to continue and I walked out of the room with the copy in hand.

As I walked to the audio building, which was across the street and half a block away, I was thinking how bad it felt to have these meetings behind Mr. Takei's back. I walked into the audio plant and approached Mr. Takei's office. The door was open as usual, and, he was standing behind his desk looking down at some papers.

I knocked on his door and, with some trepidation, I said, "Mr. Takei, I would like your opinion on something, may I come in?"

Mr. Takei looked up at me and stared. Our relationship had become uncomfortable since the announcement that I would succeed him. I knew that my promotion to Plant Manager had something to do with the hard feelings, but I wasn't sure why. After all, I had not participated in the decision making process and I was as surprised as anyone, to be named Mr. Takei's successor.

Mr. Takei didn't answer. I repeated my question, but when, once again, I received no response, I approached his desk and placed the paper with the organizational chart on his desk.

I said: "Mr. Takei, we are working on an organizational chart for MFD (micro floppy disc) and we're stuck." I had circled the problem areas. "I would like your opinion on the chart, especially the sections in the circled areas. We want to provide MFD with strong management without weakening audio."

Mr. Takei did not take his eyes off of me for several seconds. Finally, after a very long and uncomfortable pause, he looked down at the chart. He studied it for a second before sitting down and putting on his glasses. After about ten seconds, he grabbed a pen and wrote down a name and made another minor adjustment. He looked over his changes a final time, then stood and handed me the paper.

I looked at the changes he had made. They were perfect. That's it, I thought to myself. I thanked Mr. Takei and walked hurriedly out of his room. During that entire exchange, he did not say a single word. I excitedly walked back to our meeting. When I entered the crowded room, the discussion had not progressed at all. I asked the group if I could jot down some ideas. Of course everyone agreed. I altered the organizational chart on the white board according to the changes Mr. Takei made on the paper copy. It only took a few seconds. I stood to one side so that everyone could see the changes. I immediately heard someone say, "That's a great idea!" I could tell from the responses that the majority seemed to agree that the amended org chart was now complete.

Someone in the group asked, "Where did you go?"

But before I could answer, another person commented in a very futile tone, "Yes, it's a great idea but what good is it if we can't get Mr. Takei to agree?"

"These changes came from Mr. Takei." I said, "These are his suggestions, therefore, he will support them."

I heard murmurs of surprise.

Kuni asked, "Is that where you went? You went to see Mr. Takei?" He said that with a smile on his face. I think Kuni understood that it was not comfortable for me to approach Mr. Takei, yet he appreciated that I made the effort to break the ice.

After that day, I brought all major ideas and considerations from the group to Mr. Takei. His demeanor changed from the distant person back to his normal cheerful and boisterous self. After two weeks of my asking his opinion on matters he said to me, "You don't need to ask me for my opinion anymore. You know what you're doing. Just do it."

Mr. Takei stopped calling meetings for the rest of his term. He spent a lot of his time walking the plant, talking to the people and encouraging them in his jovial and playful way. Mr. Takei was very well liked.

We held a farewell party for Mr. Takei in March. A party was something that did not seem possible only a few months before. Everyone seemed to enjoy the party, especially Mr. Takei. At the end of the close of the evening, Mr. Takei went up to the microphone to speak. He thanked the people for the party and for the support they had given him over the years. He truly loved living in the U.S. He ended his speech by saying: "It is very important that each and every one of you support Walter Morita to your fullest. He is your Plant Manager now. Give him everything in your power to make him successful. If Walter is successful, California Plant will be successful."

With Mr. Takei's departure to Japan, the clock started running. California Plant was now in my hands. I had to turn things around and do it quickly. I would miss Mr. Takei, but I also had a lot of reliable help. I felt good about how things ended between Mr. Takei and I. In fact, we remain friends to this day. I learned a very valuable lesson: an essential ingredient of good leadership is building respect and mutual trust. If you can do this, then you can work your way through any problem. The second lesson that I learned was to trust my instincts, trust my heart. I learned that if it doesn't feel right, then it's probably wrong. And, some of the very best decisions that I made in my career came from my heart, not from my head.

I was about to begin my journey to improve my leadership capabilities. I knew that the skills and experience I had gained to this point were not enough to take me forward successfully. But what else did I need to know? What else did I need to change? In what ways did I need to change? How do I reach the workers?

A Strong Hand

Clearly incremental, gradual improvements would not be enough for our situation. We had to make major changes and make them quickly. I realized from the beginning that in order to pull this off, I needed to change personally. Before being appointed the new Plant Manager, I was the Director of Production Control and Purchasing. If the California Plant was not operating to TDK Japan's standards, then I must be part of the problem.

I am by nature a quiet person. California Plant needed someone vocal who could clearly and convincingly communicate the seriousness of our plant situation to all employees. To accomplish that task, I had to break out of my own comfort zone. I took two different approaches; one approach for management and a different approach for the production workers. I called the meeting with the managers and supervisors the "wake up and smell the coffee meeting."

Wake Up and Smell the Coffee

I held a weekly Manager and Supervisor Meeting that typically lasted an hour. I wrote the agenda on the white board prior to the meeting. I expected everyone to be prompt. After a few meetings into the new business year, it was clear that everyone was operating with no greater sense of urgency than before. In fact, people seemed relaxed; too relaxed. Part of the problem was my fault. My calm demeanor was working against me. I needed to do something out of character. I decided to hold a special meeting with no agenda other than a short speech I had prepared.

When the meeting room was full, I saw smiling, slightly curious faces, full of wonderment as to what I had called them in for. This was my first "special" meeting.

I began by saying that, "I will make this meeting brief. I have a few very important points to make and I will not be taking any questions. Just listen, and think about what I'm about to tell you."

I was blunt.   "If any manager or supervisor gives anything less than their full effort, I will fire him," I began.

The room instantly grew quiet. "Furthermore, if any manager or supervisor does not achieve the expected results within the specified time, I will fire him."

No one spoke.   "No second chances.   No exceptions. If you need help or if you believe there are extenuating circumstances that keep you from accomplishing your goals, you must report them to me immediately. I will not be patient any longer. Many of you in this room are operating as if we have unlimited tomorrows. I already made it clear to you that we don't. Perform, or you're out. That's all. This meeting is over." The meeting lasted only a few minutes.

I looked around the room as the managers and supervisors slowly rose and left the room. I could hear them talking in the hallway after they exited the conference room.

Rick Kline, one of my stronger managers, lagged behind the others and said: "Good speech boss. It was needed."

I didn't say anything. I was relieved. In my mind, if I didn't express clearly the serious situation we were in, if I didn't get the leaders of our organization to push forth with maximum effort, we would lose. It was a difficult thing for me to do, but it was essential. More importantly, I meant every word.

Most of the people in that room "got it."* The next step was to take the message to the rest of the workers. I tried a different approach for the hourly workers; one that I would use again and again.

---

* I had to fire a few employees who didn't "get it." It was my practice to have face-to-face meetings with problem employees so that I could directly explain clearly what my expectations were. I gave them an opportunity to turn it around. But there were a couple of managers that purposely said south when I pointed north. I had no choice but to let them go. Because terminations are confidential, firings are never announced. But people got the message when certain individuals no longer reported to work.

Taking it to the Shop Floor: The Wage Comparison Chart

Now it was time to address the production workers. When you have several tiers in the organization and hundreds of people working for you, you can't be sure how your message is communicated down the organizational chain of command. There's a certain amount of filtering, picking and sorting, differences in emphasis and, unfortunately, outright distortions. In some cases my words never reached the workers on the production floor. I had to change that. I needed to explain to the people clearly the situation we were in. I had someone interpret in Spanish everything that I was about to say. Bilingual presentations became the norm for all important messages to the production workers.

I prepared a bar graph on a slide and showed it on an overhead projector.

"This chart compares the wages of workers in different parts of the world," I began explaining, "and in fact, wages in those countries where our primary competitors have audio plants— Mexico, Thailand and China." The height of each bar represents the hourly wage of workers in the U.S., in comparison to these other countries. For example, if we are paying about $10 per hour here at our plant, a worker in the same position would make $1.50 per hour in Mexico, including fringe benefits, $1 per hour in Thailand, and, in China, $0.50 per hour.

I explained that it was crucial that we drive our factory cost down so that it matches or is lower than the factory cost in Thailand plus the cost of shipping to the U.S. If we don't achieve that goal, our machines will be shipped to Thailand and our plant will close.

But how can we do that if our wages are ten times higher than in Thailand, 20 times higher than China, where some of our competitors have moved their plants?

I heard someone say, it can't be done. Impossible said another. It can be done, I said, and I explained how.

We are very fortunate working for a company, TDK that has built its reputation on producing quality products—the best performing audio cassette tape in the world. If TDK was interested in producing the cheapest cassette possible, our plant would have closed a long time ago.

The cost of labor is only part of the total cost of producing the cassette. In fact labor constitutes less than half the cost. Material, including the tape itself, costs more than labor. To keep our factory cost low, we must also reduce the cost of material. That includes two parts: the purchasing price of the material and yield. The purchasing department must work hard on getting the best price possible for the parts. You can help drive the cost of producing a cassette down by working hard on improving our yield. Make the product right the first time. For example, if you increase the yield in molding by 1%, we can produce an extra 100,000 parts per month with the same amount of material since we are producing 10 million parts per month.

Our machines cost money also. But you can help reduce factory cost by working hard to improve machine utilization. That means, keeping the machines running well so that they produce as many "quality" parts as possible. We all have a hand in eliminating or reducing waste, and keeping our machines running. Our engineers are continually looking for ways to further automate our machines. As we automate our lines, we require fewer workers, and, we've been reducing our workforce through attrition, not through layoffs.

Finally, you must work safely. If you have an accident, you get hurt, the company gets hurt, and we all lose. Safety first. I want to be very clear: we will not achieve our goals by putting our workers at risk. As we strive to improve productivity, we will concurrently work hard to make this a safer work environment.*

There is another element in the total cost of the cassette that we don't have to worry about, but one that our competitors must add to their cost of doing business in the U.S. Our competitors must add the cost of shipping from wherever they are located to the U.S. This is a significant advantage that we have.

* I personally investigated each and every accident. I talked directly with the person who got hurt and with the injured worker's supervisor. Most of the injuries were minor--pinched fingers that resulted from a worker trying to unjam a machine without first turning it off. I explained I would not tolerate that type of unsafe activity. I would not boost our production numbers while risking the welfare of our employees. If I had to write up workers who did that, I would. By following up on each accident, I got to know more people, and they got to know that I was concerned about their well-being.

The feedback I received from the managers and supervisors was that the production workers "got it." What's more, they appreciated the fact that I told them straight up and in an adult and professional way. They understood the meaning of the bar graph. They understood what we needed to do to remain competitive.

In the next two years our workers established dozens of monthly production records in total output, yield, and machine utilization. If you added it up across molding, assembly, packaging and slitting (the process where the media was spliced together to form pancakes), the records approached one hundred.

Kuni Matsui wrote monthly reports to TDK Japan that clearly communicated our rising success, and, after a while, TDK personnel in Japan no longer spoke of closing our plant.

But as our plant regularly produced 10 million or more cassettes per month with steadily rising, yield and productivity, another huge problem loomed. Our workers weren't running out of gas, but our machines were. Our mold dies were approaching their productive life cycle. Our older assembly lines were in need of overhaul. We would need a huge investment in new equipment if we wanted to keep the plant operating, and we would need it soon.

But before we go there, let me take a slight detour and explain projects, outside of work, that brought huge rewards--disaster relief efforts united our workers and helped me to connect with the workers beyond anything I had expected.

Disaster Relief Efforts

It started off innocently enough. I read in the papers that there was a gas explosion in the city of Guadalajara, Mexico that resulted in people getting killed and injured. I initiated a canned goods and clothing drive. The response was huge. The workers at the plant were very giving people. It is true that the people with the least give the most. Our people filled a dozen gaylords (a large corrugate box measuring approximately 3' x 3' x 3'). We held a similar drive when a terrible earthquake hit Mexico City. I recall a drive for flood victims in Guatemala, and for our own Southern California town of Northridge, when a big earthquake hit. Our people never failed to respond with great generosity. We even did a drive for riot victims after the Rodney King beating touched off looting and burning. We started a drive to help the people who lost their homes through arson. However, this particular drive started slowly. I didn't understand why until a worker asked me during our monthly meeting, "Mr. Morita, we were wondering why you want to collect food and clothes for rioters?"

"Do you think the rioters burned down their own homes?" I asked. People laughed at that, and the drive turned out just as successful as all the others. I really enjoyed the fact that a worker felt comfortable enough to stand up in a crowded cafeteria and ask me that question. A breakthrough in communication had been made--open communication in both directions—going up and down the organization. Relief drives for worthy causes became one of our plant's signature characteristics.

Chapter Two:

If the bird doesn't sing . . . make it sing!

Building the Organizational Infrastructure

By the 1990's, Japanese manufacturing technique was lauded as among the best in the world, and served as a benchmark for American manufacturers. Business sections of bookstores were filled with insights into Japanese management methods. TDK's manufacturing plants embodied the best of those techniques—that is, in Japan. Transplanting that technique overseas to foreign soil and with non-Japanese workers was another matter altogether. TDK's effort to transform its U.S. workforce into something resembling the workers in Japan fell short of expectation. TDK Japan managers and engineers that volunteered to work in the U.S. often ran into culture shock. The workers in the U.S. did not respond as a Japanese worker would. One obvious difference was language. It was extremely difficult to translate abstract ideas and techniques, training concepts, teaming concepts from Japanese to English, especially to a multi-cultural workforce that consisted of many people who spoke a primary language other than English. Significant cultural differences were also in play. TDK California Plant's workforce diversity made the challenge to unite people seem impossible. The challenges went beyond language differences, as we shall see in this chapter. To make up the "slack," the TDK Japanese working at TDK California Plant simply worked harder as individuals to make up for what could not be achieved as a team. While the Japanese work ethic was tremendous and admirable, what was needed was cross cultural teamwork.

Even with TDK's enormous wealth of manufacturing experience in Japan, Japanese management did not know how to fully harness and unleash the power of the diverse American workforce. What's more, a few of the Japanese managers grew frustrated with the attempt, and, on occasion, blamed the workers as being incapable of learning complex concepts, and, as a group, less talented and dedicated than the workers in Japan. I needed to somehow make a breakthrough and come up with a way to train our workers to work more as a team and at a higher level of performance than they have been able to achieve so far.

Two new employees joined our organization and they both proved to be indispensable to this transition—that is, from stage one to stage two. First, Mr. Nobuhiro Sato arrived from TDK Japan to head the micro floppy production. Mr. Sato was an engineer by training and he quickly became one of my greatest allies, both in terms of personal support and in terms of taking care of business, i.e., leading the micro floppy business. He made a great addition to the team.

Next, I hired Jill Gray as our Human Resources Manager. We needed someone who could develop training strategies to improve the performance of all personnel, including me. Jill stayed with me for the next ten years. She had the energy and commitment to move mountains. My executive management team was now complete: Kuni Matsui in planning and production control, and the main liaison with TDK Japan, Mr. Nobuhiro Sato, heading our critical micro floppy manufacturing and Jill Gray, our new Human Resources Manager. Mark Endo, a home grown Japanese American, like myself, made up the last of the directors group that help shape our organization for the future.

In 1994, we hired a consulting firm to conduct an organizational assessment. We needed to work smarter, not just harder, but how? Where do we begin? Meanwhile, Kuni was putting together a proposal to TDK Japan for much needed new equipment. But it was questionable whether TDK headquarters would bankroll a new set of equipment that would cost millions. Worldwide audio cassette demand was slowly eroding, but we hope to convince headquarters that there was still merit in maintaining a plant in a large market like the U.S.

The conclusion of the organizational assessment was that there were three main areas where the California Plant needed to improve were communication, role clarity and accountability.

In order to systematically tackle role clarity, we needed to more clearly define each job. Even among the directors, we did not agree, for example, on the role of mechanics. Controversy over this one position, more than any other, divided the Japanese and the Americans. There were many obstacles preventing our workforce from function at the same level as the workers at TDK's Japanese plant. The antagonism and years of conflict between the Japanese engineers and the American mechanics presented a formidable obstacle, therefore this issue deserved closer attention.

Mechanics in Japan functioned very differently than mechanics here in the U.S. The American mechanics (many of whom were Hispanic) and the Japanese engineers were almost always at war. The Japanese engineers considered most of the mechanics incompetent. The American mechanics considered the Japanese engineers arrogant, standoffish and poor communicators. So it went on for years. This rift between these groups seemed irresolvable, with a history of conflict dating back to the early days of the plant.

The different manner in which the Japanese Engineer and the American mechanic approached routine mechanical problems was at the heart of these two warring groups. Prodded by the "old school" supervisor and or manager, the American mechanic would go for the quick fix. They would get the machine up and running as quickly as possible to maximize production, or so the thinking goes. On the other hand, the Japanese engineer would study the problem, arms folded, looking upstream and downstream, thinking, analyzing and thinking some more. The impatient supervisors and mechanics thought this was a waste of time. What were the engineers thinking about, they wondered? Fix the damn machine, the Americans thought, and let's get on with it. But the Japanese engineers were looking to see if the cause of the problem at hand came from somewhere upstream, and, they were trying to determine if the problem affected anything further downstream. They were trying to get to the root of the problem, rather than going for the quick fix. They were analyzing the entire process. However, the Japanese engineers never explained it to the mechanics in that way. To the Japanese engineer it was the obvious thing to do and didn't require explanation. On the other hand, the Americans, not being good at mind reading, thought the standing around and looking at the machine was a waste of time.

In order to achieve role clarity, the executive team decided that there was no other way but to hammer out all key job descriptions together. Kuni, Mr. Sato, Jill, Mark and I sequestered ourselves off site with the purpose of hammering out a consensus on the basic aspects of each major job description. Jill brought flip charts. After we completed a job function, she would tear out the page and tape it to the wall so that we could all see the progression of our work. The toughest one was the mechanics. Kuni and Mr. Sato explained the situation between the American mechanic and the Japanese engineer as I previously described. How can we get the mechanics to think more deeply? How can we get them to refrain from the quick fix and look for deeper solutions?

As we tried to work out the details of the job description for the mechanic, Jill recognized part of the dilemma. She said that the role Kuni and Mr. Sato were describing for the mechanic was actually the job description for a "technician," by American standards, i.e., a higher functioning mechanic. Just like that, the light bulbs went on. After listening to Mr. Sato and Kuni describe what the Japanese engineers that work on the production lines were actually doing, Jill said that they are not engineers. They are functioning as technicians. American technicians understand the meaning of seeking root cause and avoiding the quick fix. Therefore, we created a new job description for "technicians." We realized that the best of our mechanics in each department did function like a technician. Not all of our mechanics went for the quick fix.

But this was just part of the problem. Another aspect of the problem was the mechanics reported to the production supervisors who were responsible for meeting the production targets. The supervisors were under pressure to maximize production. We solved this problem by shifting the mechanics to report to the engineers.

This organizational change did not sit well with the production managers at first, however, when they saw the conflicts diminishing and the machine utilization rates begin to rise, they stopped complaining. We created different grades of mechanics with the best mechanics promoted to technicians. Engineers and technicians were to modify and improve the machines. Mechanics were to fix the machines, under the guidance of either a technician or an engineer. Over time, the Japanese engineers worked less and less on trouble shooting assignments and spent more of their time on making improvements. They were happy and the mechanics were happy. The war finally ended.*

After four days of intensive discussions, our executive leadership group reached a consensus on all the major job descriptions and we were ready to go to the next step.

With the help of an outside consultant, Jill Gray created a tiered pay system. We were committed to pay market rates, and all future pay increases were to be based on performance, and not length of service. We completely restructured the pay scale that, up to this point, gave the larger increases to the people who were here the longest. We stopped that practice of pay raises largely based on seniority—a practice deeply rooted in Japan. If you were here only a year, but contributed a great deal, under the new table you would get a larger increase than someone who contributed less but was with TDK longer.

---

*The Japanese engineer who, in my book, was best at breaking down communication barriers between the Japanese and the mechanics was Shinji "Shane" Higuma. Shane transferred to our Plant around 1996. His English wasn't that good, but he had excellent engineering skills. He spent hours trying to communicate difficult concepts to any mechanic interested in learning. How? I would see them in the cafeteria, huddled over a piece of napkin, as Shane would draw pictures to explain mechanical concepts and ideas. The mechanics loved him for his patience and his desire to teach them to better themselves. The desire to communicate clearly outweighs the ability to speak English.

With the help of an outside consultant, Jill Gray created a tiered pay system. We were committed to pay market rates, and all future pay increases were to be based on performance, and not length of service. We completely restructured the pay scale that, up to this point, gave the larger increases to the people who were here the longest. We stopped that practice of pay raises largely based on seniority—a practice deeply rooted in Japan. If you were here only a year, but contributed a great deal, under the new table you would get a larger increase than someone who contributed less but was with TDK longer.

Jill found a more suitable performance appraisal system. She initiated training for everyone required to assess personnel. All workers were required to give a self-evaluation. Supervisors were required to talk to their subordinates if the self score and the supervisor's score deviated significantly.

Employees were held accountable for their work now that we had clearly defined job descriptions for all position. In just a short time, Jill led the charge to improve role clarity and, together with the other directors, we were determined to hold all

workers accountable in a fair and consistent manner. This accountability included rewarding the better contributors with the higher pay increases.

Communication improved as all of the directors took the time to carefully explain each and every step we were taking. We also worked hard to keep open door policy. My door was always open for any employee who wanted to talk to me. Frankly, very few took up the offer. I initiated round table meetings where supervisors hand-picked workers from different departments and different shifts, no more than eight at a time, to have coffee and snack with me for an hour where they could ask me anything they wanted to.

I also started to walk the production floor more. We called this practice "managing by walking around." I tried to walk through every department on every shift at least once per week. We were running 24/7 and our production and warehouse had spread out to multiple buildings (seven different buildings at our peak). I tried to make eye contact and greet everyone I saw. I also tried to talk with the supervisor of each department for at least a few minutes. The workers really like to see me do this. It made them feel important, especially if I greeted them with a good morning or good evening. Managing by walking around really works. Give it a try. It may not be comfortable in the beginning. As I mentioned before, I am generally a shy person, but I was determined to break out of my comfort zone if I thought it would help me become a better leader.

Kuni prepared a business proposal calling for $14.7 million dollars investment in our plant consisting of combination of used, but still good, and new equipment. To justify this type of expenditure, we had to come up with a payback of less than 3 years through personnel reduction (through attrition), increased productivity and yield. This was 1994 and already some of our competitors were dropping out of the audio cassette business. According to our marketing department, all of our major competitors had relocated their manufacturing outside of the U.S. to Mexico or offshore. Worldwide audio cassette market was still very strong, but gradually declining. However the demand was more than enough to justify production in the U.S. provided we kept our market share. With TDK's strong sales team, maintaining a strong market share was not a problem.

We realized that to payback nearly $15 million investment in less than three years would require a radical change in the way we work. Once again, we turned to Jill Gray. We needed to train our personnel, from top to bottom, but it would cost a lot of money; money that we didn't have. We could not afford to have our workers attend training sessions while trying to payback the investment at such an aggressive rate. The solution was to turn to California's program to subsidize training for workers in order to keep businesses from abandoning the state, as many of the aerospace businesses had done. The State established a panel called the Educational Training Panel (ETP) to grant and administer the training monies. To qualify, we had to go before the panel and make a case for giving us the money. To facilitate the training, we contracted with the newly established training division within Deloitte and Touche. Deloitte and Touche, in turn, hired a local group, Bolero Associates, to conduct the training.

A proposal was drafted and we made an appointment to meet before the ETP. On the appointed morning, we met at hotel in Costa Mesa where the meeting with the state panel was to convene. The meeting was scheduled from 9 a.m. and it was scheduled to continue until all presenters were heard. We were told that each presenter or group of presenters had no more than 15 minutes to make their case before the panel.

Our presentation team met for breakfast 8 a.m.—an hour before the presentations were to begin. The meeting room was next door to the hotel restaurant. Jill and I were joined by two of the D & T administrators, John and Mary (not their real names). Just as our food was served, Mary turned to me and said, "How long is your presentation?"

From the stunned look on my face, Mary realized I didn't know I was to speak.   She turned to John.

"I thought you told him," Mary said to John.

"I thought you told him, John said to Mary.

I was dying.   I did not feel comfortable speaking in public.   My method for overcoming my apprehensiveness was to prepare, prepare, then prepare some more.   As the Plant Manager, I had to make my share of presentations, but I never grew comfortable talking before a group.   The thought of speaking before the State Panel in a packed auditorium without preparation made me ill.   I couldn't finish my breakfast.

After an awkward few moments of silence, Mary said: "Just tell the panel a little about the plant and why we need the funds and John and I will take it from there.   You can do that in your sleep."   I did not find her words comforting.

Jill tried to reassure me that I would be fine, while I sat there wishing for an earthquake; just a little one to postpone the meeting.   It didn't come.

9 a.m. rolled around quickly and we made our way into the meeting hall. It was packed. There were probably over a 100 people seated before the panel. I looked at the printed agenda. I estimated that with 15 minutes per speaker, my turn would come up around 11:30 a.m. My mind raced frantically to think of what to say. The first speaker was called and he walked up to the middle of the auditorium where an overhead projector sat. He was wearing an expensive three-piece suit and he carried an expensive leather brief case. He pulled out the slides and gave a very detailed 15 minute presentation about how the ETP funds would be used to train the workers at this business and the expected improvements as a result. His business would be that much more successful and he would remain in California, paying his appropriate share of taxes, employing good Californians for a long, long time. He was good. I hated him.

My heart was pounding and I couldn't think straight. My brain was frozen. Finally, around 10 a.m., my mind shifted towards the people back at the plant. I recalled how they wished me good luck as I departed this morning. I thought about how hard they worked and how many production records the workers had established. I thought about the $15 million investment TDK Japan was going to make in our plant based on a 3 year payback, which, in turn, depended on getting the ETP training funds. We were asking the State for $650,000 in training. It would cost us about $350,000 out of our pocket to pay for the training. In other words, we would get a $1 million worth of training for a third of the cost. It was an 18 month training process at the conclusion of which our managers and supervisors would know how to lead high performance work teams, and our workers would know how to function on these work teams. All I had to do was to stand before the Panel and tell them why we needed the money.   But I had no charts. I had no data. I had no slides.

When my name was called, I thought only about not letting the people at the plant down. Jill sat to my right. John and Mary sat behind me. I glanced at the large chandelier hanging over the middle of the room. It was perfectly still; there was going to be no earthquake this day. This is a summary of what I said that morning.

> "Ladies and gentlemen of the ETP, I thank you for allowing me to speak to you today. My name is Walter Morita. I am the Plant Manager of TDK's audio cassette manufacturing plant just down the street in Irvine. Recently, our parent company, TDK Japan agreed to invest

$15 million in new and used equipment for our facility at a time when all of our major competitors have abandoned the U.S. for Mexico and other points offshore. In exchange for the investment, which will give us new life as our equipment has become antiquated, we must pay back the loan in three years or less. And in order to do that, our workers must learn to work in a new way.

To convince our parent company, TDK Japan, to invest in our plant, our workers worked extremely hard these past two years. They have set more than 100 production records, through sheer effort. But, as I mentioned, we cannot work the same way when the new equipment arrives. Our workers need training.

There's no doubt in my mind, that we can achieve this payback schedule. But it matters to me how we do it. I could always hire new workers, already possessing some of the skills we need. But, it is important to me that when we cross that finish line three years from now, Rick, Danny, Maria, Juan, Tavo and all of the others that worked so hard to get us to this point . . . are there with me at the finish line. I don't want to stand there with a plant full of strangers. To accomplish that goal, I need your help. We need the ETP funds to train our people."

My little speech met with dead silence. For several seconds no one spoke. Jill tapped my arm and whispered, "Good job."

The panel leader finally spoke. He said, "Mr. Morita, first I want to thank your parent company for investing in your plant. Second, I commend you for your loyalty to your workers. Just how do you propose to train the workers? What kind of training is required?"

Jill nudged John and Mary, who were sitting behind me all this time. They stood up to explain the training content and process. I slumped in my chair relieved. At the end of the day, our request was approved. We got the money. From that day on, whenever I got in a tough spot, my thoughts would turn to the many people whose tireless effort got us to this point. My success as a Plant Manager was a result of their good work and I will never forget it.

The training spanned 18 months and involved everyone in the organization, from top to bottom. We formed a Quality Council to oversee the training progress. Mr. Sato, Kuni,

Jill, Mark and I made up the Council. The idea was that once the training was nearing an end, everyone in the plant had to be part of at least one high performance work team to explain his or her results. They needed the approval of the Quality Council before they could proceed, therefore, each team had to submit a proposal which included:

- A statement of the problem
- Method of data collection
- Analytical approach
- Solution
- A cost benefit ratio

The Council did not expect every project to yield great benefits. We were satisfied that everyone was participating on a project that would improve his or her work area, even if the improvement was small. However, we required at least a 3:1 cost benefit ratio, that is, the benefit would outweigh the cost by 3 times.

As a graduation exercise, each team would present their results to the Quality Council. Teams could consist of up to 8 or 9 employees. There were over 30 teams. Managers and supervisors were sponsors, i.e., they provided the resources that the team needed. But for a select group, a pre-training workshop was designed. This workshop was absolutely critical for our success.

Patricia Tappen-Koppel

Bolero Associates found a most remarkable person to conduct the pre-training. Her name was Patricia Tappen-Koppel. Patricia held dual citizenship--from Mexico and the U.S.

As a trainer, Patricia found it was common for factory workers from Mexico to be fearful of and resist the type of training we were about to embark on. The formation of high performance work teams required active participation. Some of the workers were fearful because their formal education ended after the eighth grade, the legal minimum in Mexico. They thought of the training as going back to school and they were afraid they would flunk. In addition, they were afraid to express their opinion about their work area, Patricia explained. Her pre-training program involved showing the workers how a company works. Each group would elect a plant manager, production manager, etc. They would be given exercises on running and operating a company. The pre-training required participation, which Patricia was good at eliciting. Only those workers who wanted this pre-training would receive it. It was strictly voluntary. About 50 workers signed up for it. Not all of them were Hispanic, but most of them were. The majority were women.

Patricia asked me to speak for a few minutes to each group at the end of the training. She said that it was important to them to hear from me directly why I wanted them to participate in the training. Patricia shared with me a story told to her by one of her trainees; one of our more outspoken employees. The story is one that I remained with me to this day. .

Comments from one factory worker:

> I've been working for TDK for 15 years. I'm almost 40. In all that time my supervisors never cared what I thought. Each day when I return home from work, I check on my daughter who is 15. She has a new boyfriend and I pray to God that she doesn't get pregnant. I pray to God that my son, who is 16, doesn't join the gang that hangs around our neighborhood. I tell him to stay away from those people. My husband just got laid off again, but he expects me to prepare dinner for him after working all day at TDK. When I tell him to make his own dinner, he threatens to beat me. My daughter doesn't listen to me. My son doesn't listen to me. My husband doesn't listen to me. And, for 15 years my supervisors at TDK didn't listen to me. Now, Walter is telling me, that what I think is important? He wants me to

contribute my ideas in the work place? Why? Why now?

That story was a reality check that hit me right in the gut. I gave it a lot of thought. When it came time to address each class, I needed to address this woman's question because, although she was the only one to voice her opinion frankly and openly, there were others that felt the same way. Why am I asking for ideas and opinions now, after so many years?

I made the same speech at the end of each of the pre-training workshops. My words were translated into Spanish as I spoke. Here's summary of what I said.

> First, I want to thank all of you for participating in this workshop. I can tell from your smiling faces that you really enjoyed it. Second, I want to thank Patricia. She is truly a gifted person who knows how to release the power within each human being that enters her class. Thank you Patricia.
>
> Why do I want our workers to receive the training? For years, most of the production workers here at this plant were treated as extensions of the machines. You were doing repetitious work on the production line because TDK hadn't figured out how to automate that part of the machinery. However,

did you know that in Japan, workers are expected to contribute their ideas? Their ideas are valued. Japanese workers actively participate in making their workplace better. Then, why are things done differently in California? The answer: language barrier. Communication. The TDK Japanese did not know how to train you to do the things that workers in Japan were trained to do. It was not because they wanted to treat you differently.

I heard that some of you might think you don't have valuable ideas to contribute. That is not true. Let me give you just two examples. I heard, and you tell me if is not true, that some of you, perhaps many of you, can walk into the assembly room or the packaging room, and, by listening to the sound of the machines, you can tell if you are going to have a good production day or a bad day. Is this true? I hear laughter and I see nodding heads. It must be true. I also know that many of you know which mechanics can fix the machine right so that it doesn't break down right away, and which mechanics are not as good. You are happy when Raul comes to your line to fix a problem because you know he will fix it right and fix it quickly.

You cringe when . . . well, I will not name names. But you know who is not as good as Raul.

The training we are about to receive involves showing you how to work on problems with a team of your fellow workers. You will be trained to identify which problems are worth fixing and which are not. You will learn how to solve those problems together. In this team environment, your ideas will be required.

Now, I heard a rumor that some of you think that the training is a trick to get rid of some of the workers, that is, TDK will fire workers who fail the training. This is not true. I'm telling you directly, face-to-face, this is not true. The only way you can fail the training is if you don't try. But that's true of all things in life. If you don't try, you fail. Try, and you will succeed.

Your ideas are like gold nuggets buried in the ground. With the training you are about to receive, those nuggets, your ideas, will be uncovered and put on display. As I look around this room, I see buried treasure—all of you sitting before me today. You are our future. Let's share our ideas together.*

Without Patricia's pre-training, the outcome would have been completely different. The resistance from our production line workers could have derailed the entire training process. But with her help, the majority of the workers looked forward to the training with a combination of anxiety and curiosity. The walls continued to come down.

Without Jill Gray's tremendous effort, the training would not have happened. She worked incredibly hard to ensure that the training was done, done right, documented correctly, and, that we were compensated for every dollar we were granted by the ETP.

*Years later Jill ran into a former TDK worker on the street, somewhere in Irvine. After greeting each other warmly, Jill asked the woman how she was doing. She replied that she was glad she ran into Jill because she wanted to thank her for the training she received. It had completely changed her life. She said her kids are in college. Jill exclaimed that that was wonderful. The woman continued that she finally threw her husband out of the house. When Jill looked surprised, the lady laughed. He deserved it, she said.

When Jill told me the story, we both didn't know quite what to make of it. We obviously didn't want the training to breakup anyone's marriage. But on the other hand, the boundaries of empowerment need not be limited to the workplace. This woman was truly liberated by her training experience. Dozens of workers told us that the training was life changing.

The high performance work teams were bearing fruit even as the training was going on. We paid back the $14.7 million dollars in less than 3 years. In fact, by the beginning of the 3rd year, it was a forgone conclusion, and no one talked about the payback.

The Annual Kickoff Meeting

In March of each year, we held a Kickoff Meeting at which time I would announce the major objectives for the next business year. In March 1997, the first annual kickoff after we had completed the training, we invited plant managers from other U.S. plants and key people from our NY Headquarters to attend. The meeting was to end with a special presentation by one of our star high performance work teams. The Quality Council had selected a team from Mr. Sato's micro floppy disc group to present their team project and solution.

The group from micro floppy department worked on increasing the yield of fancy boxes, made from paper, designed to hold ten 3½ inch floppy discs. The production line was constantly jamming, boxes were creased and unusable and machine utilization was unacceptable. The dozen members of this team determined that the fancy box supplier had to hold to tougher tolerances and adjustments were made to the machine. The result was an astonishing increase in fancy box yield and machine utilization. On the day of the presentation, everyone was wearing their Sunday best, and, with hands trembling, each person gave part of the presentation that led to a significant improvement in the workplace. The audience consisted of all supervisors, managers and special guests. After the MFD presentation, Eva Patterson, one of the key presenters, awarded me with a stuffed white tiger. After thanking Eva, I asked her if she chose a white tiger because I'm prematurely gray. She laughed, as did the others. It was a great day.

As I was getting ready to leave the meeting room, Mr. Sato asked me if I was going straight home, or returning to the office. I said I was going back to the office for a few minutes. He said he wanted to talk to me. I was curious, but I did not ask him what he wanted to talk about.

Mr. Sato and I shared the same office. He began by saying that he had supported me 100% throughout the training. I wholeheartedly agreed and I thanked him. He wasn't finished. He said he supported me without completely understanding what the training was trying to accomplish. But when he saw his group, workers from his MFD area, making a problem solving presentation today, he understood that the training was about a QC Circle. In other words, we had accomplished here in the U.S., what the Japanese workers were doing in Japan—workers at the California Plant were teaming to produce measurable improvements in the production area that translated into reduced cost. He had tears in his eyes when he thanked me. I didn't know what to say.

Angela Mora

Participating in disaster relief support had become an integral part of our plant work culture by the time we started our high performance team training. Two of these efforts stand out in my mind. The first of these two came in 1995 after the Kobe, Japan earthquake.

One of the production workers came to me in the cafeteria and asked if we were going to do a drive for the earthquake victims in Japan. I told her that we have already contacted the Red Cross and we were told that they needed money and not the usual food and clothing that we gather. She urged me to do it anyway.

I contacted our TDK people in Japan. Fortunately no TDK employee was killed or injured by the earthquake, although some parents of some of the workers had homes that suffered damage. Therefore, we started a drive to collect money to give directly to affected TDK family members impacted by the earthquake devastation. During one of our manager and supervisor meetings, Mitch Abellaneda announced that one of the workers in the molding production area, Angela Mora, donated her entire paycheck. We were all stunned. Most of the workers lived from paycheck to paycheck. I asked Mitch to talk to Angela and ask her to reconsider. That was much too generous. He said he already tried to talk her out of it but she insisted. Why is she giving so much, I asked? Mitch said he asked her that too. Her answer was that the Japanese had given her so much by providing a steady job and a good place to work, that she simply wanted to give back something in return.

My direct supervisor at the time was Mr. Tsuji, the President of our division--TDK Electronics Corporation (TEC). Mr. Tsuji had previously invited me to accompany him to Japan to attend the annual all-TDK business meeting held in Tokyo. When I told Mr. Tsuji that we were taking up a collection for the families of TDK workers, he said they were doing the same in NY. I told him the story of Angela Mora in molding donating her entire paycheck. Mr. Tsuji suggested that I hand the money over directly to the people at the corporate headquarters since I was going there. He would notify the Human Resources Department at TDK headquarters that we were coming.

We collected several thousand dollars. Our accounting department wrote a check for the donated amount. I had the check in my suit pocket as Mr. Tsuji and I made our way to TDK headquarters. I felt a little jet lag as we walked through the 5th floor office area. For the most part, the floor was open space with rows of desks facing each other. At the head of each row was the single desk of the section head, facing the row of workers. Only a few people, primarily Directors and up had individual offices along the outside edge of the floor. There were no partitions separating the desks.

I saw a man who appeared to be in his early 50's emerge from his office and quickly walk toward Mr. Tsuji and me. Mr. Tsuji must have told the receptionist to call him. He was the Director of Human Resources, the top ranking HR person in the corporation. He wore a warm smile as he exchanged greetings with Mr. Tsuji and I.

Mr. Tsuji looked genuinely excited as he turned to me and said, "Go ahead and tell him the story."

I said that I have a check for the money the workers at TDK California had collected to go to the families of the TDK workers that suffered from the Kobe earthquake. While Mr. Tsuji translated from my English to Japanese, the HR Director never took his eyes off of me. He was absolutely beaming.

I continued my story. I told the Director about the woman in molding, Angela Mora, who donated her entire paycheck. I said that the reason she gave for her generous gesture was because she was so grateful to work for TDK and to the Japanese who gave her the job and took care of her. The Director did not speak English, but I could tell he understood what I said even before Mr. Tsuji finished translating. With my last few words, the smile left his face and tears came to his eyes. His lips trembled as he fought to say a few words, but no words emerged. After a few seconds, he simply bowed his head and accepted my check with both hands. His simple gesture spoke volumes. I felt at that moment that a bridge had been created, not just from me to him, but across six thousand miles of ocean, from a hard working Mexican worker who grew up poor in an agrarian setting and a university educated Japanese corporate executive –two people who couldn't be more different, but at that moment, their hearts were one.

Sasha Caravejo

In 1996, we began another drive, unlike any of the ones before. My wife Carrie teaches kindergarten. A former student of hers, Sasha Caravejo, was stricken by leukemia. Her parents had started a bone marrow drive through the American Red Cross. Rafael and Ana Caravejo, Sasha's father and mother, had heard my wife speak about the many fundraisers and food drives at TDK and he asked her if she would ask me to have our plant participate in the bone marrow donor campaign. Carrie did and I agreed. Sasha was 8.

Our HR department, headed by Jill Gray, led the campaign. I was to be the contact person with the Caravejo family and with the Red Cross. A number of employees enthusiastically got into the bone marrow drive campaign. Fred Tapia, the HR Supervisor and David Boston, the Safety Manager took leading roles. We even made a little video to show our workers. Posters of young Sasha were placed on bulletin boards throughout our many buildings. The procedure was to sign up as many people as we could, and, at the appointed time, the Red Cross would send a phlebotomist to draw blood that was needed to find a match, not just with Sasha, but with anyone else in need of a bone marrow transplant. Donors with blood characteristics (i.e., markers) that matched the patient's characteristics would be called on to give a life-saving sample of their bone marrow. The process was not painless, and there was some risk to the donor.

My contact with the Red Cross informed me that a company of our size, about 500, including temporary workers, would need just one phlebotomist. One skillful phlebotomist can draw blood samples from 40 people per hour and for our company a good turnout would be 10%, or, 50 participants. I asked what would happen if more than 50 signed up, and the Red Cross contact replied confidently, don't worry, that won't happen.

In the beginning of the campaign, the signups progressed very slowly. After more than a week, we had only a couple of dozen names on our sign-up sheets. I was disappointed. During my managing by walking around the production floor, I asked one of the Hispanic supervisors why he thought the turn out was so low. He replied that Mexicans don't like to donate anything that has to do with body parts. They don't donate blood or bone marrow. It's part of the culture, he explained. I said that I had not heard that before. Meanwhile, the sign up rate continued to creep along. It appeared that the Red Cross representative was right; we would be lucky to sign up 10% of our workers.

At the end of the workday, about two weeks into the drive, I was reading emails going back and forth between our evening supervisors when one particular email caught my eye. One of the MFD supervisors informed another that he signed up almost everyone on his crew. The next day, the recipient of that email boasted that he achieved 100%, and he copied all supervisors with his memo. The next few days, I read emails going back and forth between supervisors boasting about their rate of signups.

When the total signatures raced past 80, I called the Red Cross contact and asked her for a second phlebotomist on the day of the blood drawing. She refused. She said that there's no way we are going to get more than 80. I had previously told her that to minimize production downtime, I could not allow more than 2 hours of work time for this activity. Again, she reminded me that a good phlebotomist could handle 80 in that time. She would not budge.

I called Rafael Caravejo, Sasha's father. I told him that our drive was going well and if he could give me a name of another Red Cross contact. I did not want to use the rep assigned to me any longer. Rafael said he would call the Red Cross and have someone contact me right away. The next day I received a call from a new contact from the Red Cross. She was as friendly and positive, as the first one was negative. She had no problem getting me a second phlebotomist. But by the time she called me, the number of signatures had exceeded 120, therefore, I asked her if it became necessary, would I be able to get a third? She responded, "By all means." Just let her know if we need another phlebotomist. The following day I called her for a third phlebotomist. With only a few days before the blood drawing, the number of signup had exceeded 200. The number kept rising.

It seems that the reason for the slow initial response was that the bone marrow drive required a lot more explanation than any of our previous drives. This was understandable because what was required of the donor was much more than simply donating food, clothing or money. The supervisors who took the most time to explain the purpose of the drive and what was to be expected, got the best response. Communication was the key.

Finally, we approached the eve of the event, the number of signatures exceeded 250. I needed a fourth phlebotomist. My contact agreed to send four the next day, but now even she sounded skeptical. Are you sure, she asked? Yes, I said firmly. I know these people. If they say they will participate, they will.

When the day of the blood drawing arrived, four phlebotomists showed up, as promised. They were all professional and courteous. We set up for tables with chairs in our largest conference room. At the appointed time, workers began lining up. I was near the front of the line. Kuni was not far behind. The line stretched and stretched in a serpentine manner as each production area sent a few workers at a time. We did not stop production. When the last of the workers had his blood drawn, the total reached 350—that is, 350 out of 500 workers, including temps. We had achieved a staggering bone marrow donor signup rate of 70%.

When the news reached Rafael Caravejo, Sasha's father, he couldn't believe it. Rafael was an engineer for a large company. At his place of work, they reached 10%. He said 70% was unheard of. "You don't know our people," I replied proudly.

A few weeks later we received word that Sasha had a match. No, the match was not from our group. But, never the less, we were all happy for her. She was to get a new lease on life. Without the donor, she would have died within a short time. Sasha was eight years old when we did the drive. She survived until a month before her high school graduation. She was a brave little girl with a terrific attitude and a big heart. Her courage touched many people.

Chapter Three:

If the bird doesn't sing . . . wait until it does.

High Performance Work Teams

After the training, supervisors and managers regularly formed high performance team projects throughout the year. When a team finished one project, they started another. Each employee was required to participate in two projects per year. Jim Tetiva, an outstanding supervisor, regularly led multiple projects continuously throughout the year. He did not have to be reminded to start a new project. Factory cost continued to go down. The $14.7 million investment had been paid off long ago. The plant was profitable. Morale was high, but we could never ease up on our effort to improve. Being content was a luxury that we could not afford. Worldwide demand for audio tapes continued to decline, but TDK's sales department worked hard to increase market share to make up the difference. Our plant continued to make as many cassettes as we could produce. Our mold die maintenance group came up with a method of maintenance that lengthened the lifespan of our dies. Our plant was highly unlikely to receive another large investment in our equipment, therefore, we had to make whatever we had last for as long as possible. For example, the normal life span of a mold die for injection molding was one million shots. Our mold maintenance crew designed a procedure to achieve two million shots. Then three. Amazing!!! And, we did not back off on our quality requirements.

Mr. Sato returned to Japan about a year after the training was completed. Ironically, a few years later, Mr. Sato was assigned to be the Plant Manager of the Thailand Plant. I was happy for him. He was very deserving.

Kuni Matsui transferred to the NY Headquarters office, and I hated to see him go. After about a year in New York, Kuni Matsui was promoted to President of TDK Electronics Corporation and he became my boss. Kuni was an extremely capable person and I was lucky to have him at my side for six years. His promotion was well deserved. Now, as the President, he was a California Plant ally. As such, Kuni negotiated with the Parts Division of TDK. Up to that point, TDK kept its Parts Division and Media Division separate. Kuni negotiated the production of E.L. Coil (a coil inductor part often used in automobiles) at our facility in Irvine. We were in three buildings now, down from a peak of seven. The Audio Cassette Plant remained where it was, as did the Micro Floppy Disk production plant, just a block from Audio. In 1995, we moved our warehouse and distribution a half mile away into a very large 400,000 sq. ft. building, of which we occupied 300,000 sq. ft. In 1997, a production room was built for the E.L. Coil manufacturing in this building. As we did with MFD, we carefully selected very capable people to work and manage the lines. Because of its proximity to the packaging department, Danny Hennes was appointed the Senior Manager of both E.L. Coil and Packaging.

In September of 2000, Kuni called a meeting in New York. I traveled to NY monthly to meet with Kuni and other senior TDK executives, therefore, I was expecting a routine meeting. Jill accompanied me on this visit. She was now the senior HR person in our organization. It was at this September meeting that Kuni dropped the bombshell news: TDK Japan had decided to close the audio plant. Worldwide audio demand had dropped to a point that from a global standpoint, it made sense for TDK to meet its worldwide production requirements from only one location—Thailand. The audio plant in Germany was to close at the same time as the plant in California.

Kuni added that unfortunately, we couldn't keep E.L. Coil production without audio. Therefore, E.L. Coil production would shutdown first, at the end of January 2001. Then, in March, at the end of the fiscal year, the audio plant would close. A group of people, primarily engineers, will remain to dismantle the machines and ship them to Thailand. Obsolete or unneeded equipment was to be sold or scrapped. Only packaging and warehouse distribution would remain in California. I was assigned to find a suitable new location for a packaging and distribution center.

Kuni asked me how I wanted to handle the announcement to the workers in California. Still reeling from the news, I said I would call a meeting with the managers immediately after I got back and announce the news to them. I immediately heard a lot of skeptical comments from the senior American executives regarding my intentions. "Why do you want to tell them so soon," asked one of the NY executives? "Don't you think the workers will get mad and sabotage the machines? What's the rush? Wait until it's closer to closing."

"No," I said. "I need to tell them right away so that they can prepare for their future." Again, I heard a lot of negative feedback. Finally, Kuni intervened. He told the group that Walter has a special relationship with the workers in California. "I will allow him to handle it as he wishes."

Kuni then turned to me and said, "But you need to achieve the business plan. Do you understand? It is your responsibility to hit all of your target numbers all the way until the plant closes."

"Yes, of course," I replied. "I will achieve the business plan." I thanked Kuni for his trust in me. It meant a lot. Kuni was with me in the trenches in California for six years, including shortly after I was named Plant Manager. I owed a great deal of my success to him. Kuni knew that I had developed a strong level of respect and trust with the workers at the plant. It was my call and I was very grateful to have it, as awful as the message was. If we were going to close the plant, we were going to do it in a way consistent with the way we've operated to this point—openly and honestly. But even I did not foresee what was to happen.

After the meeting, I asked Jill to arrange a meeting of all of the managers and supervisors for a "special session" upon my return.

A Very Special Meeting

As the managers and supervisors walked into the conference room, my thoughts turned to the "wake up and smell the coffee meeting" held years ago. Back then, we didn't know if our plant would remain open for six months. Here we were, more than eight years later, at the peak of production and still profitable. As I looked around the room, I saw curious, smiling and unsuspecting faces. It is my custom to start the meetings right on time, and everyone was punctual.

I got right to the point. "A decision has been made by our headquarters in Japan to close our plant. Worldwide audio cassette demand has diminished to the point that it would be most efficient and cost effective to consolidate all of the tape production into one plant, Thailand, for the remaining life cycle of the product. We are closing the plant through no fault of our own. We accomplished everything asked of us, and more. For years, our plant has met and exceeded expectations placed on us, but this is still a business and the decision to consolidate plants makes business sense."

I went on to explain the timetable: "EL Coil would close first, at the end of January 2001, followed by audio at the end of March 2001. A small crew of primarily mechanics and engineers will remain until June 2001 to dismantle machines that were being shipped to Japan or Thailand, and to help move equipment that will be sold. Less than one-fourth of the 350 workers would remain to operate the packaging and distribution center, which will be at a new site somewhere in this vicinity."

I explained that the criteria for selecting who was to remain as part of the packaging and distribution group would be based on who best met the needs, based on performance appraisals and skill set, for all of the positions remaining. We would not keep anyone, no matter how good, if they did not have the right experience and skills.

In the next two to four weeks, we will let everyone know if they will be a part of the remaining group or not. If we offer a position to someone who turns it down, we will ask the next person in line. Severance packages that are fair and consistent will be given to everyone who remains until the end, but will not be given to anyone leaving before the scheduled end date.

I asked if there were any questions. Someone asked if there was a chance that the decision could be changed. I said no. Another person asked why E.L. Coil had to shut down, and I said because we cannot keep the E.L. Coil cost down if we layoff all of the engineers and indirect support that Coil requires.

When the questions stopped, I asked the group when and how we should make the announcement to the rest of the workers. I was met with silence. After a few seconds, I saw people looking around to see who was going to speak next. Someone blurted out, "we can't tell them yet."

"Why not?" I asked. "They deserve the same courtesy that I've given you."

I believe it was Dan Hennes who spoke next, "We can't tell them now because we're not ready."

"That's right," said Jill, "we have to prepare a plan."

"I agree," said Rick Kline. "We should have a plan on how we are going to help them, before we make the announcement."

Brenda Holley contributed to this plan, as did Mark Endo and Ross Masud, the Engineering Manager. I was floored. I just told these employees, people with car payments and mortgages, that 75% of them would be without a job before next June. But here they were, thinking about their fellow workers. Jill walked to the board, and the group began a brainstorming session.

"We can schedule two job fairs before Coil closes," said Jill. "One at the end of October and another one in December."

"Training, we need to offer training," someone said. "I heard companies were hiring people with soldering skills for integrated circuits."

"Yeah, I'm sure German Guttierez and Mark Stephens would be glad to teach a workshop," someone interjected. (Both German and Mark volunteered their own time for these workshops.)

We will help every worker prepare a resume. We will list all of the process improvement teams that they worked on.

We can have workshops on interviewing. Most of our people have been with us for so many years that they need to practice going to an interview.

And at the end, we can have a big party, someone suggested. That was another one of our signature traits—we always celebrated our successes and important milestones. Why not celebrate the end of a great era?

And so it went on for 45 minutes. I sat there, without saying a word, watching these great people prepare a plan, just like they would for a high performance work team project. I was never prouder of our leadership group. I had just witnessed an amazing display of unselfish devotion by our managers and supervisors to the people that worked for them. I suppose a negative person may say that this discussion was less about benefitting others and more about self-preservation. That is, the managers and supervisors did not want to announce the closing without a plan. This is true to an extent. Perhaps you had to be there and witness this discussion to see that it went well beyond just self-preservation.

A beautifully constructed plan was prepared in a little over a week. Once again, Jill took the lead. All the pieces were in place for the big announcement.

There was no way to make the announcement to all workers at the same time. Our workforce was spread out in such as way that we decided to have two people make the announcement. I was to make the announcement at our Distribution Center, and Mark Endo, the Director of Production, was to make the same announcement at the audio building. We picked shift change time so that workers arriving and workers leaving could hear the announcement at the same time. I'm sure Mark would agree, it was the toughest speech either of us had to make.

I explained the three critical phases of shutting down. The E.L. Coil workers were in the Distribution Center, and they heard me say that they were the first to go. Unknown to me at the time, a group of coil workers gathered together for a secret meeting, shortly after the announcement.

I explained the preparation for layoff plan that Jill and the managers and supervisors had diligently worked on. I could tell from the look on some of the faces that a few were in shock. They probably didn't hear much after I said "shutdown" and "layoff." When I finished, I asked for questions. I received none.

The workers slowly dispersed. However, one person stayed behind and approached me. It was Ed Pollard, one of our skillful plant maintenance workers. I must confess, I did think he might vent on me, or worse yet, throw a punch. Instead, he stuck out his hand. Surprised, I extended my hand to meet his. Ed simply said, "Thank you for trusting us by giving us so much notice. We won't disappoint you." With that he turned and walked away.

Yes there were tears and bitterly disappointed people, but for the most part, the news was accepted with calm disappointment. During the next few weeks, Jill and I went over the list of who we thought would make the best fit for the remaining distribution and packaging center. We met with each person selected, and then we met with each one that was not chosen to remain. In two weeks, everyone knew where he or she stood. There was no sabotage. There were no work slowdown or protest meetings. We hit all of our business plan numbers until the last day, including the bottom line. On the production lines, it was business as usual, with one truly remarkable exception.

E.L. Coil

E. L. Coil production was halfway through its 3rd year in September 2000, when I announced the plant closure. We had a good group of workers working the line. The production room was in the Distribution Center, adjacent to our packaging lines. Senior Manager, Danny Hennes, was in charge of both E.L. Coil and Packaging. Although the production numbers were quite good, the department had not been able to achieve the assigned target of 98.5% yield. In the coil division, achieving 98.5% was a strong indicator that the department was functioning well. This yield target was a world-wide TDK components division benchmark. Although the department reached and exceeded 98.0% several times, we could never quite get to 98.5%.

October 2000 was the first full month of production after the closure was announced. Therefore, I waited with anticipation at our monthly production meeting in November to hear the production results from each of the production areas. I had promised Kuni Matsui that we would achieve our business plan. I had been checking the numbers periodically, thus, I was not expecting any big surprises. The accounting department had already informed me that we achieved our factory cost and profit numbers for October. I was not expecting a drop off in our primary production and yield numbers.

When it came time for Dan Hennes's report, we were all expecting a routine presentation. Danny, reading from his notes, reported that the E.L. Coil department achieved its production target. Machine utilization was on target. There were no accidents. And, the yield for the month was 98.5%.

I stopped him there. "Danny," I asked, "What did you say the yield was?"

Danny looked up at me, then down at his report and he repeated, "It's 98.5%! We hit 98.5%," he said excitedly as he suddenly realized the significance of the number.

"How did you do that Danny?" I asked.

"I. . . I don't know?" Danny replied.

"Please find out."

"I will," said Danny.

"Please make sure it's not a mistake," I added.

A week later, during another meeting, Danny informed us that the E.L. Coil group had indeed hit the target of 98.5%. It was not a mistake.

"How did they do that, after all this time?" I asked.

Danny explained that after the plant shutdown was announced, a group of the E.L. Coil workers secretly gathered together and decided that they were going to hit the yield target before their last working day. They met with the mechanics and formulated a plan. They didn't tell anyone just in case they were unable to make it.

"They didn't tell you or the supervisors?" I asked.

"That's right, the supervisors didn't know either," Danny responded.

The Japanese E.L. Coil engineer, Kenichi "Ken" Inoue, calculated the yield and he crosschecked it against the number of rejected parts. The yield figure is correct.

October the yield was 98.5%, and in November, December, and January, the final months of production, the E.L. Coil department exceeded 98.5%! This was a tremendous achievement. Jill Gray was enrolled in a graduate HR program at the time. She researched to see if there was a precedent for workers improving their production area after a layoff was announced. She could not find any. The only exception she could find was where a group of factory workers achieved a production record because they hoped it would forestall the layoff. That was not the case here. I made it very clear that E.L. Coil would close at the end of January.

I prepared a Certificate of Achievement for all the workers in that department. On the left side of the certificate, there was a graph that showed both the production output and the yield figures rising over time. A star was affixed next to the date of the layoff announcement, so that the reader could see that the yield target was achieved AFTER the announcement. Affixed to the right side of the folder was a copy of a letter addressed to a recruiter or HR personnel, stating that this worker achieved something truly phenomenal—breaking a production yield record after being notified of a lay off. I hoped this Certificate would help all of them land a job.

I was once asked, years later, what did I think of the fact that Danny Hennes did not know that the production line workers were secretly meeting to push the yield up over the 95% threshold? My answer was simple. Danny Hennes was one of the best managers I had. Although the Coil group was the first to face the layoff, there was no sabotage. There were no disgruntled employees. Danny had trained and empowered his workers extremely well. He simply waited for the birds to sing—and sing they did.

The Last Day of EL Coil

We created a Reward and Recognition Committee (R & R) made up of about 8 or 10 members, about the time we started our team training. Half the members were from Human Resources and the others came from different departments. I asked this committee to help organize the activities for the last day for E.L. Coil workers.

The Committee worked on the Memory Book, which is what we called it, that was modeled after a high school yearbook. It contained group pictures of all of the departments by shift, and individual pictures. The last half of the book contained a collage of photos of employees taken over 27 years of TDK California Plant history. We left blank pages for the workers to write little notes and comments to their departing friends. Jill organized a contest for the Memory Book cover design and Supervisor Octavio Navarro's artwork was selected. Workers were asked to bring in photos. It was a labor of love. Once we received the finished product each worker was given a Memory Book.

Jill hired a mariachi band to perform that day. Managers and supervisors were scheduled to cook, BBQ chicken and steak. We ordered salad, rice and other side dishes.

I told Jill that I didn't want to make a speech. I wanted to do something different. Of course I would say a few words, but only a few. I asked the R & R Committee to join me in a song that we would sing together to the departing E.L. Coil workers. After we had our lunch, the E.L. workers hurriedly sat in the front two rows of chairs set up in the cafeteria in the Distribution Center. The other workers sat behind the coil workers. I stood on the dais with my fellow R&R Committee members. I had selected the song De Colores ("*The Colors*").

I explained to the audience that this was a happy song well known among the people in Mexico. I welcomed the workers to join in once we began. I explained that this song captured the spirit of hard working people all over this land and it seemed to me to be appropriate for this occasion.

I looked down at the smiling, eager faces before me. We began to sing…

"De Colores, de colores se visten los compos en la primavera . . ."

(In colors, in colors, the fields are dressed in the spring . . .)

That was as far as we got when everyone in the first two rows burst out crying. The Committee continued to sing.

"De colores, de colores son los pajaritos que vienen afuera . . ."

(In colors, in colors are the little birds that come from outside . . .)

Row after row of workers started to cry, cascading from front to back.

"De colores, de colores es el arco iris que vemos lucir . . ."

(In colors, in colors, is the rainbow that we see shining . . .)

By the time we finished the song, there was not a dry eye in the cafeteria. The mariachi band backed us up during our singing and the band members were pretty misty eyed too.

That concluded the farewell party. Workers tearfully hugged their friends and gradually everyone drifted away.

The R & R Committee used a similar format at the end of March when the audio plant closed. We decided to skip the singing on that occasion. One of our supervisors, Octavio Navarro, gave me a tribute, and said some very nice things about me, but frankly, I was too bummed out to listen. It was a tough day for all of us.

I had kept my promise to Kuni. We achieved our business plan. The California audio plant hit all of its key performance targets and was profitable until the factory doors closed.

Conclusion

Walking through an empty manufacturing plant is a lot like walking down the halls of a school in the summer when school is out. I can almost hear the sound of lockers banging and the sound of people walking quickly to their workstation at the start of the workday. I can visualize people lining up to clock out at the end of their shift, anxious to get back to their families for a few hours, before returning for another day of work. I can almost hear the laughter and noisy chatter in the cafeteria filled with hungry workers and I can almost smell the tortas, enchiladas and tacos warming up in the microwave. I can see the maintenance technician extraordinaire, Craig Shappy, replacing filters in an air conditioning unit. There's Rick Kline rolling up his sleeves to help the mechanics with a particularly tough mechanical problem. There's Brenda Holley with her near perfect recall beaming as she rattles off the names of Japanese engineers that worked here 20 years before. Ken Seider is working on his quality control procedures. The building still houses the spirit, energy, sweat and toil of hundreds of workers working endless hours for nearly three decades.

Jill said it best on that last day when she spoke to the departing workers. She said: "This is not your last day. This is the first day of your life after graduating from the University of TDK. Life goes on, just like it did when you graduated from school. Now you will embark on a new adventure, a new chapter in your life, armed with the knowledge and experience you gained while working here."

As usual, Jill was right.

Appendix: Lessons learned

The bottom line is still the bottom line—in any business, the most important thing is to make money. But it makes a difference how you make the money and the way you lead is the key to your success.

The extent to which you are able to harness the power of your workers will be the measure of your leadership ability. To unleash the power of your employees, you must empower them. Concurrently with empowering the workforce, you need to provide clear direction.

Mutual trust is the key to empowerment. Trust is implicit in empowerment and it is the fundamental building block required to maximize the human potential in your organization.

Every leader must find a way to develop mutual trust and respect with his employees. I built it by making it my practice to speak to the workers openly and honestly. I took an interest in worker safety and I engaged the employees in charitable drives. You have to find your own way.

Leadership must be flexible. You must know when to apply a strong hand and when to stand back. This is true for both the organizational level and the individual level.

Some of you may find that you are inhibited by the boundaries of your comfort zone. You may not feel comfortable exerting a strong hand. Or, conversely, exerting a strong hand comes easy for you, but it is difficult to express yourself openly and honestly before a large group. We all have a comfort zone. If yours is keeping you from being the leader you want to be, tell yourself, as I did, if I want the workers to give 100%, so must I. If you expect the workers to push through their comfort zone to achieve their target, you should do no less.

Organizations go through stages. You must adjust your leadership style to match the stage. If you take a strong hand in a Tokugawa stage (3rd stage) you will create chaos. If your approach is too soft in a Nobunaga stage (first stage), you will be ineffective. This is true on an individual basis. Some workers require a strong hand, even if the organization, as a whole, is in the 3rd stage. Some workers require very little guidance, even in a start up stage.

Leadership must be flexible on an individual basis as well as on an organizational level. You must not take a strong hand with a very capable person, even in a Nobunaga stage. Conversely, you must take a strong hand with poor performers, even in a Tokugawa stage.

When you come to a fork in the road and you don't know whether to go left or go right, follow your heart. The best decisions I made came from the heart. Trust your instincts.

Remember, the overwhelming majority of workers want to do a good job and want to feel proud of their accomplishments. As a leader, it is your job to show them how and to provide them with the resources to be successful.

No matter how busy you are, spend part of everyday thinking about the future. The person at the top of the organization should be thinking about the future more than 50% of the time. If you're not thinking about the future of the organization, who is?

Build a strong team of co-leaders. Don't be afraid to let these key people lead, as long as it's not in a different direction. Delegate important responsibilities to these key people. Work hard at giving them the resources they need to be successful. Succession planning is a 3rd stage process.

Try managing by walking around. Unless you have hundreds of people working for you spread out in multiple buildings, you should make an effort every day to walk through your work place. Make eye contact with everyone. Stop and talk to a different person each day. You will be surprised how much you will see that you never saw before. The workers will perceive you differently also. Above all else, they will see that you care enough to see how they are doing.

Maintain a good sense of humor. If you're an uptight person, your organization will be an uptight organization. Stay loose. There's enough tension in the work place; don't add to it.

Be a good listener. You're never too smart or experienced to learn new things.

Lead by example. Shortly after I became plant manager, my human resources staff informed me that managers and supervisor were amassing their vacation and personal days. That is, they weren't taking time off. At the next managers meeting, I encouraged managers to take time off. Relaxation was important. A month later I approached the HR staff and asked if managers and supervisors were taking time off after I made the announcement. She said no. I asked the HR manager what was going on. She said: "Managers and supervisors are not taking time off because you aren't." I got it. At the next meeting I asked again for the management team to take some time off. I told them I would be taking a day off this week, and again a day next week, and possibly a couple of more after that. No one said anything. Another month went by and the HR staff person said that managers and supervisors were beginning to schedule time off. I learned two valuable lessons: lead by example, and, the person who is unafraid to tell you what you should hear, and not what you want to hear, is your very best ally. Jill was like that. So was Norma DiGerlando, Jill's successor.

Embrace change. Change is inevitable. If your organization remains static, your competitors will pass you up.

Reward and recognize worker accomplishments frequently. It doesn't cost money to say thank you and well done. Reward and recognize publicly. Assign volunteer staff to come up with creative ways to R & R. You will never be short of volunteers. Give them a modest budget. R & R does not have to cost much.

Celebrate your successes often. Party. Have fun. Your employees know you work under a lot of pressure. If they see that you can handle the pressure and still have fun, they will too.

Acknowledgement

I owe so much to the people who helped me throughout my career, beginning with Terry Tsutsui who took a chance and hired a guy who didn't know how to put together a decent resume, Sam Koizumi, who took a chance and trusted me to take on newer and bigger responsibilities. Sam was followed by Mr. Takei, the Plant Manager that I succeeded, and who asked every worker in the plant to give me their full support upon his leaving for Japan. When I became the Plant Manager, I reported to the President of TDK Electronics Corporation, beginning with Mr. Tsujii, followed by Mr. Kihara, then Kuni Matsui. All three gave me nothing but their full support. I deeply appreciated the amount of trust and confidence each of these three leaders demonstrated towards me.

The ten-year period that I describe in this book was an exercise in teamwork at a very high level. My thanks to the core group with whom I practiced the Japanese form of *nemawashi,* or consensus building: Kuni Matsui, Nobuhiro Sato, Jill Gray and Mark Endo. We came together as a group, and then we found a way to lead the workers in the plant from one stage to the next, and to the next. It wasn't easy.

Even after all these years, looking back, it was clearly not easy.

As a group, the Japanese expatriates who worked at our plant were true pioneers—who exhibited the spirit of adventure working in a foreign land, bringing along their spouses and children, and, working harder than any group I had ever seen or worked with. They were truly dedicated to the company, while at the same time, embracing America and the American way of life. Kazu Kuroda is one who not only supported me as my primary liaison to TDK Japan and TDK NY, but who also became a very good friend. Each year, Kazu continues to send me birthday wishes even though almost two decades have passed since we worked together.

I also admired the immigrant workers, most of whom came from south of our border, but some from Southeast Asia, China, Taiwan, and a few from Europe. These workers reminded me of my Issei (first generation) grandparents—extremely hard working with a positive attitude towards make a life and seeking opportunities in the U.S., if not for themselves, then for their children and grandchildren.

As a first time writer, it took a lot of encouragement from a handful of friends to get me to finish this book and get it published.

Those dear friends include George Kometani, shiatsu master and former aerospace engineer. George knows full well what a bad manager looked like because he worked for a few. Thank you George, for your kind words of support. Many thanks also to Cedric Scott, Hollywood producer and dear friend. Cedric, as busy as he is, took the time to read my work and got back to me with suggestions and encouragement. Dr. Noelani Hong, PhD has been a long time supporter of my writings. Thank you Noe for your friendship and unwavering support. Very special thanks to my daughter-in-law, Radeyah Morita, who helped to edit this work. I needed your extra set of eyes, and your good advice. Thanks to my friend Frank Sweeney, a lawyer extraordinaire, current CEO of TDK U.S.A, who took the time from his busy schedule to read my book and offered me invaluable advice.

Last, but not least, I thank my family—my wife Carrie, and my sons Ty and Greg. I worked long hours during my career with TDK, and I traveled a fair amount both domestically and overseas. It was always a struggle to balance my time with my family and my career. Therefore, I appreciate your love and support throughout my career.

Made in the USA
San Bernardino, CA
27 February 2020

65032978R00071